CW00523975

The ID16™© Pe

The Administrator. Your Guide to the ESTJ Personality Type

The Advocate. Your Guide to the ESFJ Personality Type

The Animator. Your Guide to the ESTP Personality Type

The Artist. Your Guide to the ISFP Personality Type

The Counsellor. Your Guide to the ENFJ Personality Type

The Director. Your Guide to the ENTJ Personality Type

The Enthusiast. Your Guide to the ENFP Personality Type

The Idealist. Your Guide to the INFP Personality Type

The Innovator. Your Guide to the ENTP Personality Type

The Inspector. Your Guide to the ISTJ Personality Type

The Logician. Your Guide to the INTP Personality Type

The Mentor. Your Guide to the INFJ Personality Type

The Practitioner. Your Guide to the ISTP Personality Type

The Presenter. Your Guide to the ESFP Personality Type

The Protector. Your Guide to the ISFJ Personality Type

The Strategist. Your Guide to the INTJ Personality Type

Also by Jaroslaw Jankowski

Who Are You?
The ID16™© Personality Test

Which of the sixteen personality types is yours? Are you an energetic and decisive 'administrator'? A sensitive and creative 'artist'? Or a dazzling and analytical 'logician', perhaps?

Who Are You? offers you the ID16™© Personality Test, along with an outline of the sixteen personality types, including essential information on their natural inclinations, potential strengths and weaknesses, related types, and an overview of how often each type occurs in the world population. Armed with what you discover, you'll understand yourself and others far better!

Why Are We So Different?
Your Guide to the 16 Personality Types

Why are we so very different from one another? Why do we organise our lives in such disparate ways? Why are our modes of assimilating information so varied? Why are our approaches to decision-making so diverse? Why are our forms of relaxing and 'recharging our batteries' so dissimilar?

Your Guide to the 16 Personality Types will help you to understand both yourselves and other people better. It will aid you not only in avoiding any number of traps, but also in making the most of your personal potential, as well as in taking the right decisions about your education and career and in building healthy relationships with others.

The book contains the ID16™© Personality Test, which will enable you to determine your own personality type. It also offers a comprehensive description of each of the sixteen types.

The Practitioner

Your Guide
to the ISTP Personality Type

The Practitioner

Your Guide
to the ISTP Personality Type

The ID16™© Personality Types series

JAROSLAW JANKOWSKI
M.Ed., EMBA

This is a book which can help you exploit your potential more fully, build healthy relationships with other people and make the right decisions about your education and career. However, it should not be considered to be a substitute for expert physiological or psychiatric consultation. Neither the author nor the publisher accept any responsibility whatsoever for any detrimental effects which may result from the inappropriate use of this book.

ID16$^{TM©}$ is an independent typology developed by Polish educator and manager Jaroslaw Jankowski and grounded in Carl Gustav Jung's theory. It should not be confused with the personality typologies and tests proposed by other authors or offered by other institutions.

Original title: Twój typ osobowości: Praktyk (ISTP)
Translated from the Polish by Caryl Swift
Proof reading: Lacrosse | experts in translation
Layout editing by Zbigniew Szalbot
Cover photographs by Shutterstock

Published by LOGOS MEDIA

Paperback: ISBN 978-83-7981-084-0
EPUB: ISBN 978-83-7981-085-7
MOBI: ISBN 978-83-7981-086-4

Contents

Preface

The work in your hands is a compendium of knowledge on the *practitioner*. It forms part of the *ID16™© Personality Types* series, which consists of sixteen books on the individual personality types and *Who Are You? The ID16™© Personality Test*, an introduction to the ID16™© independent personality typology, which is based on the theory developed by Carl Gustav Jung.

As you explore this book on the *practitioner*, you will find the answer to a number of crucial questions:

- How do *practitioners* think and what do they feel? How do they make decisions? How do they solve problems? What makes them anxious? What do they fear? What irritates them?

- Which personality types are they happy to encounter on their road through life and which ones do they avoid? What kind of friends, life partners and parents do they make? How do others perceive them?

- What are their vocational predispositions? What sort of work environment allows them to function most effectively? Which careers best suit their personality type?
- What are their strengths and what do they need to work on? How can they make the most of their potential and avoid pitfalls?
- Which famous people correspond to the *practitioner*'s profile?

The book also contains the most essential information about the ID16™© typology.

We sincerely hope that it will help you in coming to know yourself and others better.

ID16™© and Jungian Personality Typology

ID16™© numbers among what are referred to as Jungian personality typologies, which draw on the theories developed by Carl Gustav Jung (1875-19161), a Swiss psychiatrist and psychologist and a pioneer of the 'depth psychology' approach.

On the basis of many years of research and observation, Jung came to the conclusion that the differences in people's attitudes and preferences are far from random. He developed a concept which is highly familiar to us today: the division of people into extroverts and introverts. In addition, he distinguished four personality functions, which form two opposing pairs: sensing-intuition and thinking-feeling. He also established that one function is dominant in each pair. He became convinced that each and every person's dominant functions are fixed and independent of external conditions and that, together, what they form is a personality type.

In 1938, two American psychiatrists, Horace Gray and Joseph Wheelwright, created the first personality test based on Jung's theories. It was designed to make it possible to determine the dominant functions within the three dimensions described by Jung, namely, **extraversion-introversion**, **sensing-intuition** and **thinking-feeling**. That first test became the inspiration for other researchers. In 1942, again in America, Isabel Briggs Myers and Katherine Briggs began using their own personality test, broadening Gray's and Wheelwright's classic, three-dimensional model to include a fourth: **judging-perceiving**. The majority of subsequent personality typologies and tests drawing on Jung's theories also take that fourth dimension into account. They include the American typology published by David W. Keirsey in 1978 and the personality test developed in the nineteen seventies by Aušra Augustinavičiūtė, a Lithuanian psychologist. Over the following decades, other European researchers followed in their footsteps, creating more four-dimensional personality typologies and tests for use in personal coaching and career counselling.

ID16™© figures among that group. An independent typology developed by Polish educator and manager Jaroslaw Jankowski, it was published in the first decade of the twenty-first century. ID16™© is based on Carl Jung's classic theory and, like other contemporary Jungian typologies, it follows a four-dimensional path, terming those dimensions the **four natural inclinations**. These inclinations are dichotomous in nature and the picture they provide gives us information regarding a person's personality type. Analysis of the first inclination is intended to determine the dominant **source of life energy**, this being either the exterior or the interior world. Analysis of the second inclination defines the dominant **mode of assimilating information**, which occurs via the senses or via intuition. Analysis of the third inclination supplies a description of the **decision-making mode**, where either mind or heart is dominant, while analysis of the fourth inclination produces a definition of the dominant **lifestyle** as either organised or spontaneous. The combination of all these natural inclinations results in **sixteen possible personality types**.

One remarkable feature of the ID16™© typology is its practical dimension. It describes the individual personality types in action – at work, in daily life and in interpersonal relations. It neither concentrates on the internal dynamics of personality nor does it undertake any theoretical attempts at explaining or commenting on invisible, interior processes. The focus is turned more toward the ways in which a given personality type manifests itself externally and how it affects the surrounding world. This emphasis on the social aspect of personality places ID16™© somewhat closer to the previously mentioned typology developed by Aušra Augustinavičiūtė.

Each of the ID16™© personality types is the result of a given person's natural inclinations. There is nothing evaluative or judgemental about ascribing a person to a given type, though. No particular personality type is 'better' or 'worse' than any other. Each type is quite simply different and each has its own potential strengths and weaknesses. ID16™© makes it possible to identify and describe those differences. It helps us to understand ourselves and discover our place in the world.

Familiarity with our personality profile enables us to make full use of our potential and work on the areas which might cause us trouble. It is an invaluable aid in everyday life, in solving problems, in building healthy relationships with other people and in making decisions relating to our education and careers.

Determining personality is a process which is neither arbitrary nor mechanical in nature. As the 'owner and user' of our personality, each and every one of us is fully capable of defining which type we belong to. The individual's role is thus pivotal. This self-identification can be achieved either by analysing the descriptions of the ID16™© personality types and steadily narrowing down the fields of choice or by taking the short cut provided by the ID16™© Personality Test.[1] The role played by each 'personality user' is equally crucial when it comes to the test, given that the outcome depends entirely on the answers they provide.

Identifying personality types helps us to know both ourselves and others. Nonetheless, it should not be treated as some kind of future-determining oracle. No personality type can ever justify our weaknesses or poor interpersonal relationships. It might, however, help us to understand their causes!

ID16™© treats personality type not as a static, genetic, pre-determined condition, but as a product of innate and acquired characteristics. As such, it is a concept which neither diminishes free will nor engages in pigeonholing people. What it does is open up new perspectives for us, encouraging us to work on ourselves and indicating the areas where that work is most needed.

---

[1] The test can be found in *Why Are We So Different? Your Guide to the 16 Personality Types* by Jaroslaw Jankowski.

The Practitioner (ISTP)

THE ID16™© PERSONALITY TYPOLOGY

The Personality in a Nutshell

Life motto: Actions speak louder than words.

In brief, *practitioners* …

are optimistic and spontaneous, with a positive approach to life. Reserved and independent, they hold true to their personal convictions and view external principles and norms with scepticism. They find abstract concepts and solutions for the future tiresome and would far rather roll up their sleeves and get to work on solving tangible and concrete problems.

Adapting well to new places and situations, they enjoy fresh challenges and risks and are capable of keeping a cool head in the face of threats and danger. Their general reticence and extreme reserve when it comes to expressing their opinions mean that other people may often find them impenetrable.

The *practitioner's* four natural inclinations:

- source of life energy: the interior world
- mode of assimilating information: via the senses
- decision-making mode: the mind
- lifestyle: spontaneous

Similar personality types:

- the Inspector
- the Animator
- the Administrator

Statistical data:

- *practitioners* constitute between six and nine per cent of the global community
- men predominate among *practitioners* (60 per cent)
- Singapore is an example of a nation corresponding to the *practitioner's* profile[2]

The Four-Letter Code

In terms of Jungian personality typology, the universal four-letter code for the *practitioner* is ISTP.

General character traits

Practitioners live for today. With their positive approach to life and the ability to enjoy the moment, it is rare for them

---

[2] What this means is not that all the residents of Singapore fall within this personality type, but that Singaporean society as a whole possesses a great many of the character traits typical of the *practitioner*.

to worry about the future. They exist in the here and now and, in general, dislike long-term plans, duties and obligations and are unlikely to devote overmuch time to preparation, preferring to act on impulse, rather than following a series of previously formulated steps. They are aesthetically tuned, but have no fondness for the flamboyant or bizarre, and their lifestyle is relatively simple.

Perception and learning

Practitioners spot details which escape the notice of others, but struggle when it comes to seeing the wider perspective, the long-term effects of their decisions and the connections between disparate facts and phenomena. As a rule, they view abstract theories and concepts with scepticism. With their natural 'feel' for things technical and their manual dexterity, they are practical to a fault. What appeals to them is the nitty-gritty of putting things into practice ... hence the name for this personality type.

They are also more highly inclined towards risk-taking than any of the other fifteen personality types and generally number amongst those whose childhood was marked by their propensity to dismantle their toys or any device within their reach in order to find out how they were made. They often have fairly painful memories of lessons at school since they perceive dry, theoretical and monotonous tasks as tiresome in the extreme and, with their love of experiment and freedom to approach a task as they want, learn best and most readily by doing. The way things work fascinates them and, as a rule, they handle tools masterfully, carrying out all kinds of alterations, improvements and repairs with enormous skill. When solving a problem, they have the ability to zoom straight in on the equipment and materials they will need and then set to work without further ado. They excel at manual tasks and, even when doing something for the first time, may well give the impression of being experts.

Interior compass

Practitioners are flexible by nature and capable of adapting readily to new circumstances, although they are fiercely protective of their privacy and equally as firm about ensuring that no one else succeeds in organising their lives for them. They loathe being told what they should do or how they should live; indeed, on occasion, they will deliberately go so far as to behave contrary to expectations simply as a matter of principle. However, they accept criticism well and are also capable of carrying out critical appraisals of others.

Being independent in the extreme, they refuse to allow others to make decisions for them and harbour an intense dislike of being checked on and controlled. Freedom, independence and space are as necessary to them as oxygen and they are infuriated by any attempt to 'invade' their territory. At times, they can even be obsessive as far as their privacy is concerned.

In general, they are sceptical as regards widely recognised authorities and equally as dubious when it comes to norms and truths imposed from 'on high', preferring to live their lives in accordance with their own principles. On the whole, they do what they themselves believe to be right, without fretting over other people's opinions and evaluations and, being insusceptible to external pressure, are capable of standing by their convictions and predilections.

As a rule, they follow the principles of egalitarianism, believing that we are all equal and should all be treated in the same way. Titles, background and position make little impression on them, although they do respect people who have some kind of special experience or remarkable practical skill.   By the same token, the respect and admiration of others gives them enormous satisfaction and they therefore like to have the sense that they are specialists in their field.

As others see them

Others view *practitioners* as self-assured, cold and highly puzzling. Even so, in matters requiring manual dexterity or technical know-how, they come across as experts and have a reputation for being resourceful, practical people who can always be counted on. Those around them are thus often surprised by their volatility – their enthusiasm wanes quickly and they often change their mind. Their short-term view of things and their lack of interest in problems which go beyond the here and now can sometimes irritate other people, who may well also be disconcerted by their mysteriousness, reticence and reluctance to share their thoughts and opinions.

In turn, *practitioners* themselves hold no truck with anyone who tries to instruct them or exert pressure on them. People who are capable of spending months discussing far-reaching plans without taking so much as a single practical step towards turning them into reality are a closed book to them. They also have enormous difficulty in assimilating the fact that, when they and others look at the same situation and have the same information at their disposal, they will come to diametrically different conclusions.

Communication

Practitioners' reticence means that people often perceive them as mysterious and impenetrable. They rarely consult others, but are independent in making their decisions, which sometimes comes as a surprise to their nearest and dearest or colleagues. The least communicative of all the sixteen personality types, they seldom have much to say and, when they do speak, they tend to be concise to the point of terseness. More often than not, though, their contribution to the conversation or discussion is highly pertinent and absolutely to the point.

Observation

Practitioners are splendid observers and unceasingly monitor their surroundings in search of new information. Quick to spot change, they evaluate any new data they acquire with an eye to either its potential impact on their own lives or the possibility of using it to solve the concrete problems they come up against. However, they also tend to discard information which is inconsistent with their experience, an approach which sometimes narrows their view and can even give rise to a growing vision of the world which is both alternative and wholly individual in nature.

Problem solving

When *practitioners* are solving a problem, they are capable of making a rapid assessment of the situation, taking all the measures and means available to them at that moment into consideration and making an on-the-spot decision which meets the occasion. They cope extremely well if a crisis develops and improvisation or rapid decisions are called for. By the same token, when tried and tested procedures or established rules fail and other people are at a loss as to what to do, *practitioners* follow their internal compass and keep a cool head, an ability which also serves them well when essential decisions need to be made in situations of increased risk or imminent danger, since they will act rationally and objectively, heedless of the emotional reactions going on around them.

Leisure

Knowing how to enjoy life and combine work and pleasure, *practitioners* have no trouble in finding time to relax, unwind and indulge in their hobbies. Their leisure pursuits often involve their manual dexterity and they also enjoy physical activities and simply having fun. They will happily meet up with people who share similar interests and views, thus deepening their knowledge and enabling them to acquire new information at one and the same time. Although they are relatively immune to stress, prolonged periods of tension can cause them to grow cynical and embittered and may also lead to their becoming increasingly self-isolated or reacting with inordinate vehemence.

Socially

Practitioners are highly reticent by nature, which makes them very unapproachable. However, the reason behind this is not the antipathy towards people which is sometimes suspected of them. On the contrary, they are tolerant, open to others and perfectly capable of forming healthy and friendly relationships.

On the other hand, they do hold to the assumption that conversations and get-togethers should serve some kind of purpose, such as collaborating to solve a problem. Spending time with other people is not something they consider to be an end in itself and, by the same token, they view integration meetings with the same intense dislike that they feel for social gatherings and celebrations. The world of conventions and courtesies leaves them utterly baffled and they are wholly incapable of making any kind of small talk, finding it astonishing that anyone has the time to talk about nothing. In general, gatherings with strangers hold as little charm for them as talking to people with completely different interests, an activity which strikes them as tiresome in the extreme.

Practitioners often run into problems as a result of their inability to express their feelings and emotions. In general, they assume that actions speak louder than words, which is why they prefer to convey their feelings and affections by doing something concrete. When the people closest to them or their friends or acquaintances need practical help, they can always be counted on.

Amongst friends

Practitioners value simplicity and independence in their relationships with others and will often consciously avoid the kind of contact which demands a more profound emotional engagement and involves expending a great deal of energy and time. They respect other people's privacy and independence, but set just as much store by their own, and take great pains to guard their own 'territory'. They are often visited by a powerful need for solitude, tranquillity and space, which is frequently misread by others as a display of distance or a lack of interest in their needs.

However, their friends are familiar with another side of their character and, in their midst, *practitioners* are not only happy to listen to them, but will frequently shower them with questions as well. Tolerant and flexible, they enjoy a reputation of being good company, and their ability to find their feet in all kinds of situations means that they are perceived as people who are always up and doing. Their ability to derive joy from life impresses others, as does their love of adventure and thrills.

Although they can listen to people with genuine interest, they themselves say little, expressing their own opinion rarely and exhibiting an extreme reluctance to open up to others. When pressed for their views, such replies as they do give may well be evasive or enigmatic. While they sometimes give the impression of being loners, the truth is that they need other people and feel isolated and superfluous without them. They forge closer relationships with people who share similar interests and views and will frequently have no more than a few friends and acquaintances, more often than not *inspectors*, *animators*, *logicians* and other *practitioners* and, most seldom, *counsellors*, *mentors* and *enthusiasts*.

As life partners

Practitioners afford their partners a great deal of the freedom that they themselves need, since they find any attempt to limit them intolerable. They bring spontaneity and enthusiasm to their relationships, habitually focusing on the present moment and devoting little time to cogitating over what the future might hold. This is not to say that they are incapable of staying in one relationship for a lifetime, though. It simply means that their view of things is not a long-term one – for *practitioners*, every day is a fresh page. Nonetheless, given that this is their usual mode of thought, the notion of taking a vow which binds them "until death do us part" might well fill them with apprehension.

Reticent by nature, it is rare for them to voice their views, opinions and feelings. The greatest challenge they face in their relationships is the other side of that same coin; in other words, their inability to identify their partner's feelings and emotional needs, which is often mistakenly perceived as a lack of interest. They may love them dearly and yet, at one and the same time, have absolutely no grasp whatsoever of their emotions and what they are feeling and experiencing. By the same token, they can simply fail to understand that their partner needs compliments and affection. Given that they themselves have no such emotional requirements, the fact that others do can come as a shock to them and leave them confounded, since they have no idea whatsoever as to how to meet them.

When a crisis looms in their relationship, *practitioners* will normally strive to save it. However, if no results are forthcoming from their efforts, they may throw in the towel, resigning themselves to the fact that the situation has got beyond their control or concluding that their partner's demands are excessive. On the whole, they have no major problems with ending toxic and destructive relationships.

The natural candidates for a *practitioner's* life partner are people of a personality type akin to their own: *inspectors*, *animators* or *administrators*. Building mutual understanding and harmonious relations will be easier in a union of that kind. Nonetheless, experience has taught us that people are also capable of creating happy and successful relationships despite what would seem to be an evident typological incompatibility. Moreover, the differences between two partners can lend added dynamics to a relationship and engender personal development. Indeed, for many people, this is a prospect that appears more attractive than the vision of a harmonious relationship wherein concord and full, mutual understanding hold sway.

As parents

Practitioners make flexible and tolerant parents who allow their children considerable freedom and the space to develop without excessive supervision. Nonetheless, they are capable of applying discipline and doling out punishments when the situation requires it. However, they feel no obligation to instil them with their own values, explain the world to them or tell them how to live, an attitude which can sometimes mean that their offspring have little knowledge of the rules that make the world go round.

Practitioners have difficulty in engaging with their children emotionally and with taking the time to talk to them and share fun and games with them. Indeed, it may well be that they are, *de facto*, more of an absence than a presence in their lives. In effect, the relationship between *practitioner* parents and their offspring is often coloured by a certain emotional distance and can run into serious trouble if the other parent also struggles to meet this aspect of their children's needs. On the other hand, they excel when it comes to providing their children with a variety of appealing activities and, in general, they are unstinting with their money and outstanding organisers of all kinds of expeditions and trips. For the *practitioners*, these are occasions when they can get to know their offspring better and, for the children, they are the most treasured moments of their childhood and will remain engraved in their memory throughout their lives.

Work and career paths

Practitioners' enthusiasms are their key to success. When they are engaged in something they love, they can move mountains. As people of action, they like to be up and doing. Change is meat and drink to them and they quickly tire of tasks which demand lengthy concentration or planning and require them to focus on the future. To a *practitioner*, the ideal undertaking is one with a short time span.

Companies and institutions

Bureaucratised institutions with rigid structures and precisely defined procedures are a torment to *practitioners:* planning, reporting and accounting for what they do are activities from another planet as far as they are concerned. Viewing routine as a form of torture, they much prefer variety and have impressive multi-tasking skills, although they normally find starting something far easier than following it through to the end.

They fit in well in companies which give their employees freedom in carrying out their tasks rather than imposing restrictions on them, and they are at their happiest when solving concrete, tangible and practical problems. Risk and experiments hold no fear for them, although they would rather work in areas which they are thoroughly familiar with. As time goes by, they will frequently become genuine experts in the fields which interest them.

As part of a team

Practitioners are perfectly capable of collaborating closely with other people. However, in their case, this will not normally lead to their forging emotional ties with the group.

As a rule, they will be the ones who bring objectivity and realistic evaluations to the work and display the ability to analyse facts coolly and without emotional engagement.

Views on workplace hierarchy

In general, given that *practitioners* are quite capable of self-motivation and thus have no need of close supervision, they appreciate superiors who provide their staff with freedom of action. When they hold a managerial position, they are quick to discern their organisation's problems and identify the weak links. Realists by nature, they are not subject to illusion and their perception of the world around them is almost never coloured by rose-tinted glasses. Trying to persuade others and themselves that "things can only get better" and that "it will all come out in the wash" is alien to them. By the same token, they suffer no qualms when it comes to ridding the organisation of poor employees without further ado.

With their dislike of consultation and their aversion to turning to others for their opinions, they hold no brief for collegial and democratic management styles, much preferring to make their decisions independently. One frequent outcome of this approach is that they fail to delegate sufficiently and wind up overburdened as a result.

Unafraid of taking risks, making bold decisions and playing for high stakes, they will sometimes hazard everything on one throw. With no fear of difficult decisions, they are capable of acting without needing comprehensive data and neither emotion nor sentiment influence what they do. Accusations are sometimes levelled at them for failing to take the human cost into account and, indeed, their primary interest is normally the objective good of the organisation rather than the staff's feelings.

Professions

Knowledge of our own personality profile and natural preferences provides us with invaluable help in choosing the optimal path in our professional careers. Experience has shown that, while *practitioners* are perfectly able to work and find fulfilment in a range of fields, their personality type naturally predisposes them to the following fields and professions:

- anti-terrorism
- the armed forces
- aviator
- carpentry, joinery and cabinet-making
- computer programmer
- computer systems analyst
- the construction industry
- crisis management
- detective
- driver
- economist
- electrician
- electronics
- engineer
- entrepreneur
- farmer
- firefighter
- IT specialist
- jeweller
- lawyer
- lifeguard
- locksmith
- pharmacist
- mechanic
- metalworker

- musician
- police officer
- security and protection
- sportswoman/sportsman
- technician

Potential strengths and weaknesses

Like any other personality type, *practitioners* have their potential strengths and weaknesses and this potential can be cultivated in a variety of ways. *Practitioners'* personal happiness and professional fulfilment depend on whether they make the most of the 'pluses' offered by their personality type and face up to its inherent dangers. Here, then, is a SUMMARY of those 'pluses' and dangers:

Potential strengths

Practitioners are spontaneous, flexible and tolerant. As excellent listeners and observers, they spot details which escape the notice of others, using the information they acquire to build an internal database unique to themselves and then applying it to solving concrete problems. Practical by nature, they have inbuilt manual and technical skills. They are self-assured, enthusiastic and optimism is their middle name. Their approach to life is positive ... *practitioners* have the ability to enjoy every moment. Change holds no fear for them and they would always rather be up and doing. When those close to them need their practical assistance, they will spare neither time nor energy in providing it.

No matter what, *practitioners* will stand firm by their convictions, remaining insusceptible to external pressure. They can handle criticism and have no trouble in expressing it themselves or calling other people's attention to shortcomings. Capable of making decisions on the basis of partial data and acting under conditions of increased risk, they cope extremely well in situations of threat and danger, crises and rapidly shifting circumstances. When others are overcome by emotion, *practitioners* keep a cool head, making objective and rational decisions. They are unafraid of bold moves and risk, a character trait which also means that they are capable of ending toxic and destructive relationships.

Potential weaknesses

The inability to express their feelings is one of the greatest weaknesses which *practitioners* face, along with their insensitivity to the emotional needs of others, an aspect of their natures which can mean that they cause hurt without even being aware of it. Their reticence may also be a source of problems, as may the fact that they have little grasp of how to suit their mode of communication to the moment. Their loathing of any kind of supervision or oversight can lead to their becoming uniquely obsessive as regards their privacy and even to their self-isolation.

Coping with long-term tasks and strategic planning comes hard to *practitioners*, since they have difficulty in seeing the wider perspective, the long-term effects of their decisions and the connections between disparate facts and phenomena, to say nothing of assimilating complex, abstract theories. Given that they are quick to grow bored, they also find focusing on one thing for an extended period an uphill struggle and are easily distracted. As such, they tend to find starting something far easier than following it through to the end.

Inclined to dismiss anything that conflicts with their own experience, they surround themselves with people who share their interests and views, a *modus operandi* which can lead to their developing their own alternative vision of the world. Despite their openness to new knowledge and experiment in the fields which interest them, they themselves rarely step beyond the areas that they are already familiar with.

Personal development

Practitioners' personal development depends on the extent to which they make use of their natural potential and surmount the dangers inherent in their personality type. What follows are some practical tips which, together, form a specific guide that we might call *The Practitioner's Ten Commandments*.

Think ahead

You are capable of solving problems of the immediate and practical kind. However, the most crucial issues most often demand a global approach and long-term action. If you want to tackle them, you need to broaden your outlook and expand your consideration of time spans.

Give theory its due

Every time you discard something which has no immediate practical application, you call down a whole range of limitations on yourself. True, not every theory can be put to use in solving concrete problems, but they can all still extend our viewpoint and help us to understand the world. Also, never forget that they often inspire practical undertakings in the future as well!

Broaden your horizons

Test the water with things that go beyond the world of whatever you are currently interested in. Talk to people with views and interests other than your own. Undertake tasks you have never touched before. It will give you a host of valuable ideas and mean that you start seeing the world from a wider perspective.

Finish what you start

You launch into new things enthusiastically, but have problems with finishing what you have already begun, a *modus operandi* which usually produces mediocre results. Try sorting out what is most important to you and deciding how you want to accomplish it. Then knuckle down and turn your back firmly on all those tempting distractions!

Stop dismissing other people's ideas and opinions

Just because other people's ideas and opinions conflict with your own, this does not automatically mean that they are wrong. Before you judge them as valueless, give them some serious consideration and try to understand them.

Say more

Share your thoughts and ideas with others. Express your emotions. Tell people how you feel and what you are going through. You will be helping your colleagues and your nearest and dearest immensely when you do. Whatever you say, it will usually be better than remaining silent.

Treat others kindly

People have no desire to be seen as nothing more than tools serving to accomplish a goal. They long for their emotions, feelings and enthusiasms to be perceived. Mix with people, communicate with them, try to put yourself in their shoes and understand what they are going through, what fascinates them, what worries them and what they fear. Then wait and see. The difference will come as a pleasant surprise!

Stop dismissing universal principles

You make your way through life guided by your own interior compass and believing that happiness is not dependent on universal rules. Society is, though! Give some thought to what would happen if everyone ignored the principles underlying community life and began to live solely in accordance with their own, personal rules.

Ask others for help

When you experience difficulties or troubles, share that fact with people you trust. Stop hesitating when you have a problem – ask others for their help!

Keep your impulsiveness reigned in

Before you make a decision or commit yourself to something, devote a little time to gathering some relevant information, analysing it and evaluating the situation coolly and objectively. When you take that approach, you will most likely find yourself with less to do and, more to the point, you will end up doing it better.

Well-known figures

Below is a list of some well-known people who match the *practitioner's* profile:

- **Leonardo da Vinci** (Leonardo di ser Piero da Vinci; 1452-1519); an Italian Renaissance painter, architect, philosopher, musician, poet, inventor, mathematician, mechanic, anatomist and geologist, to name but some of his skills, he is probably the most widely talented person in history and is generally acknowledged as the archetypal 'Renaissance man'.
- **Michelangelo** (Michelangelo di Lodovico Buonarroti Simon; 1475-1564); a painter, sculptor, architect and poet, he was one of the greatest artists of the Italian Renaissance.
- **Charles Bronson** (Charles Dennis Buchinsky; 1921-2003); an American screen actor of Lipka Tatar and Lithuanian-American origins, his filmography includes *The Dirty Dozen*.
- **Alan Bartlett Shepard** (1923-1998); the first American astronaut.

- **Clint Eastwood** (born in 1930); an American screen actor, director, producer, film composer whose filmography includes *Dirty Harry*. He has won numerous prestigious awards and is also a politician.
- **Woody Allen** (Allan Stewart Konigsberg; born in 1935); an American screenwriter, director, actor, musician, producer, film composer and comedian whose filmography includes *The Purple Rose of Cairo*, he has won numerous prestigious awards.
- **Bruce Lee** (Lee Jun Fan (1940-1973); an American screen actor of Chinese extraction whose filmography includes *Enter the Dragon*, he was also a master of the martial arts.
- **Frank Zappa** (1940-1993); an American musician, bandleader, songwriter, composer, recording engineer, record producer, and film director, he fronted The Mothers of Invention rock group.
- **Michael Douglas** (born in 1944); an American screen actor, director and producer whose filmography includes *Wall Street*.
- **John Malkovich** (born in 1953); an American screen actor of Croatian descent whose filmography includes *In the Line of Fire*, he is also a producer, director and fashion designer.
- **Rowan Atkinson** (born in 1955); a British stage and screen actor, comedian and screenwriter whose filmography includes the *Mr Bean* television series and feature films.
- **Meg Ryan** (Margaret Mary Emily Anne Hyra; born in 1961); an American screen actress and producer, best-known for her roles in romantic comedies such as *When Harry Met Sally*.
- **Tom Cruise** (Thomas Cruise Mapother IV; born in 1962); an American screen actor and producer

whose filmography includes the *Mission Impossible* movies.

The ID16™© Personality Types in a Nutshell

The Administrator (ESTJ)

Life motto: *We'll get the job done!*

Administrators are hard-working, responsible and extremely loyal. Energetic and decisive, they value order, stability, security and clear rules. They are matter-of-fact and businesslike, logical, rational and practical and possess the capability to assimilate large amounts of detailed information.

Superb organisers, they are intolerant of ineffectuality, wastefulness and slothfulness. True to their convictions and direct in their contact with others, they present their point of view decisively and openly express critical opinions, sometimes hurting other people as a result.

The *administrator*'s four natural inclinations:

- source of life energy: the exterior world
- mode of assimilating information: via the senses
- decision-making mode: the mind
- lifestyle: organised

Similar personality types:

- the Animator
- the Inspector
- the Practitioner

Statistical data:

- *administrators* constitute between ten and thirteen per cent of the global community
- men predominate among *administrators* (60 per cent)
- the United States is an example of a nation corresponding to the *administrator's* profile[3]

Find out more!

The Administrator. Your Guide to the ESTJ Personality Type by Jaroslaw Jankowski

---

[3] What this means is not that all the residents of the USA fall within this personality type, but that American society as a whole possesses a great many of the character traits typical of the *administrator*.

The Advocate (ESFJ)

Life motto: *How can I help you?*

Advocates are well-organised, energetic and enthusiastic. Practical, responsible and conscientious, they are sincere and exceptionally gregarious.

Advocates are perceptive of human feelings, emotions and needs. They value harmony and find criticism and conflict difficult to bear. With their sensitivity to any and every manifestation of injustice, prejudice or detriment to another, they are genuinely interested in other people's problems and take real delight in helping them and tending to their needs, while often neglecting their own. They have a tendency to do everything for others and can be vulnerable to manipulation.

The *advocate*'s four natural inclinations:

- source of life energy: the exterior world
- mode of assimilating information: via the senses
- decision-making mode: the heart
- lifestyle: organised

Similar personality types:

- the Presenter
- the Protector
- the Artist

Statistical data:

- *advocates* constitute between ten and thirteen per cent of the global community
- women predominate among *advocates* (70 per cent)
- Canada is an example of a nation corresponding to the *advocate's* profile

Find out more!

The Advocate. Your Guide to the ESFJ Personality Type
by Jaroslaw Jankowski

The Animator (ESTP)

Life motto: *Let's DO something!*

Animators are energetic, active and enterprising. Fond of the company of others, they have the ability to enjoy the moment and are spontaneous, flexible and open to change.

Animators are inspirers and instigators, spurring others to act. Being logical, rational and pragmatic realists, they are wearied by abstract concepts and solutions for the future. Their focus is on solving concrete problems in the here and now. They have difficulties with organising and planning and can be impulsive, acting first and thinking later.

The *animator's* four natural inclinations:

- source of life energy: the exterior world
- mode of assimilating information: via the senses
- decision-making mode: the mind
- lifestyle: spontaneous

Similar personality types:

- the Administrator
- the Practitioner
- the Inspector

Statistical data:

- *animators* constitute between six and ten per cent of the global community
- men predominate among *animators* (60 per cent)

- Australia is an example of a nation corresponding to the *animator's* profile

Find out more!
The Animator. Your Guide to the ESTP Personality Type
by Jaroslaw Jankowski

The Artist (ISFP)
Life motto: *Let's create something!*

Artists are sensitive, creative and original, with a sense of the aesthetic and natural artistic talents. Independent in character, they follow their own system of values and are optimistic in outlook, with a positive approach to life and an ability to enjoy the moment.

Helping others is a source of joy to them. They find abstract theories tedious and would rather create reality than talk about it, although starting on something new comes more easily to them than finishing what they have already started. They have difficulty in voicing their own desires and needs.

The *artist's* four natural inclinations:

- source of life energy: the interior world
- mode of assimilating information: via the senses
- decision-making mode: the heart
- lifestyle: spontaneous

Similar personality types:

- the Protector
- the Presenter
- the Advocate

Statistical data:

- *artists* constitute between six and nine per cent of the global community
- women predominate among *artists* (60 per cent)
- China is an example of a nation corresponding to the *artist's* profile

Find out more!

The Artist. Your Guide to the ISFP Personality Type
by Jaroslaw Jankowski

The Counsellor (ENFJ)

Life motto: *My friends are my world*

Counsellors are optimistic, enthusiastic and quick-witted. Courteous and tactful, they have an extraordinary gift for empathy and find joy in acting for the good of others, with no thought of themselves. They have the ability to influence other people, inspiring them, eliciting their hidden potential and giving them faith in their own powers. Radiating warmth, they draw others to them and often help them in solving their personal problems.

Counsellors can be over-trusting and have a tendency to view the world through rose-tinted glasses. With their focus on other people, they often forget about their own needs.

The *counsellor's* four natural inclinations:

- source of life energy: the exterior world
- mode of assimilating information: intuition
- decision-making mode: the heart
- lifestyle: organised

Similar personality types:

- the Enthusiast
- the Mentor
- the Idealist

Statistical data:

- *counsellors* constitute between three and five per cent of the global community
- women predominate among *counsellors* (80 per cent)
- France is an example of a nation corresponding to the *counsellor's* profile

Find out more!

The Counsellor. Your Guide to the ENFJ Personality Type by Jaroslaw Jankowski

The Director (ENTJ)

Life motto: *I'll tell you what you need to do.*

Directors are independent, active and decisive. Rational, logical and creative, when they analyse problems they look at the wider picture and are able to foresee the future consequences of human activities. They are characterised by optimism and a healthy sense of their own worth and are capable of transforming theoretical concepts into concrete, practical plans of action.

Visionaries, mentors and organisers, *directors* possess natural leadership skills. Their powerful personalities and direct and critical style can often have an intimidating effect, causing them problems in their interpersonal relationships.

The *director's* four natural inclinations:

- source of life energy: the exterior world

- mode of assimilating information: intuition
- decision-making mode: the mind
- lifestyle: organised

Similar personality types:

- the Innovator
- the Strategist
- the Logician

Statistical data:

- *directors* constitute between two and five per cent of the global community
- men predominate among *directors* (70 per cent)
- Holland is an example of a nation corresponding to the *director's* profile

Find out more!

The Director. Your Guide to the ENTJ Personality Type by Jaroslaw Jankowski

The Enthusiast (ENFP)

Life motto: *We'll manage!*

Enthusiasts are energetic, enthusiastic and optimistic. Capable of enjoying life and looking ahead to the future, they are dynamic, quick-witted and creative. They have a liking for people in general, value honest and genuine relationships and are warm, sincere and emotional. Criticism is something they handle badly. With their gift for empathy and ability to perceive people's needs, feelings and motives, they both inspire others and infect them with their own enthusiasm.

They love to be at the centre of events and are flexible and capable of improvising. Their inclination leads towards idealistic notions. Being easily distracted, they have problems with seeing things through to the end.

The *enthusiast's* four natural inclinations:

- source of life energy: the exterior world
- mode of assimilating information: intuition
- decision-making mode: the heart
- lifestyle: spontaneous

Similar personality types:

- the Counsellor
- the Idealist
- the Mentor

Statistical data:

- *enthusiasts* constitute between five and eight per cent of the global community
- women predominate among *enthusiasts* (60 per cent)
- Italy is an example of a nation corresponding to the *enthusiast's* profile

Find out more!

The Enthusiast. Your Guide to the ENFP Personality Type by Jaroslaw Jankowski

The Idealist (INFP)

Life motto: *We CAN live differently.*

Idealists are sensitive, loyal, and creative. Living in accordance with the values they hold is of immense importance to them and they both manifest an interest in the reality of the spirit and delve deeply into the mysteries of life. Wrapped up in the world's problems and open to the needs of other people, they prize harmony and balance.

Idealists are romantic; not only are they able to show love, but they also need warmth and affection themselves. With their outstanding ability to read other people's feelings and emotions, they build healthy, profound and enduring relationships. They feel that they are on very shaky ground in situations of conflict and have no real resistance to stress and criticism.

The *idealist's* four natural inclinations:

- source of life energy: the interior world
- mode of assimilating information: intuition
- decision-making mode: the heart
- lifestyle: spontaneous

Similar personality types:

- the Mentor
- the Enthusiast
- the Counsellor

Statistical data:

- *idealists* constitute between one and four per cent of the global community
- women predominate among *idealists* (60 per cent)
- Thailand is an example of a nation corresponding to the *idealist's* profile

Find out more!

The Idealist. Your Guide to the INFP Personality Type by Jaroslaw Jankowski

The Innovator (ENTP)

Life motto: *How about trying a different approach…?*

Innovators are inventive, original and independent. Optimistic, energetic and enterprising, they are people of action who love being at the centre of events and solving 'insoluble' problems. Their thoughts are turned to the future and they are curious about the world and visionary by nature. Open to new concepts and ideas, they enjoy new experiences and experiments and have the ability to identify the connections between separate events.

Innovators are spontaneous, communicative and self-assured. However, they tend to overestimate their own possibilities and have problems with seeing things through to the end. They are also inclined to be impatient and to take risks.

The *innovator's* four natural inclinations:

- source of life energy: the exterior world
- mode of assimilating information: intuition
- decision-making mode: the mind
- lifestyle: spontaneous

Similar personality types:

- the Director
- the Logician
- the Strategist

Statistical data:

- *innovators* constitute between three and five per cent of the global community
- men predominate among *innovators* (70 per cent)
- Israel is an example of a nation corresponding to the *innovator's* profile

Find out more!

The Innovator. Your Guide to the ENTP Personality Type
by Jaroslaw Jankowski

The Inspector (ISTJ)

Life motto: ***Duty first.***

Inspectors are people who can always be counted on. Well-mannered, punctual, reliable, conscientious and responsible, when they give their word, they keep it. Being analytical, methodical, systematic and logical by nature, they tend be seen as serious, cold and reserved. They prize calm, stability and order, have no fondness for change and like clear principles and concrete rules.

Inspectors are hard-working, persevering and capable of seeing things through to the end. As perfectionists, they try to exercise control over everything within their sphere and are sparing in their praise. They also underrate the importance of other people's feelings and emotions.

The *inspector's* four natural inclinations:

- source of life energy: the interior world
- mode of assimilating information: via the senses
- decision-making mode: the mind
- lifestyle: organised

Similar personality types:

- the Practitioner
- the Administrator
- the Animator

Statistical data:

- *inspectors* constitute between six and ten per cent of the global community
- men predominate among *inspectors* (60 per cent)
- Switzerland is an example of a nation corresponding to the *inspector's* profile

Find out more!

The Inspector. Your Guide to the ISTJ Personality Type by Jaroslaw Jankowski

The Logician (INTP)

Life motto: *Above all else, seek to discover the truths about the world.*

Logicians are original, resourceful and creative. With a love for solving problems of a theoretical nature, they are analytical, quick-witted, enthusiastically disposed towards new concepts and have the ability to connect individual phenomena, educing general rules and theories from them. Logical, exact and inquiring, they are quick to spot incoherence and inconsistency.

Logicians are independent, sceptical of existing solutions and authorities, tolerant and open to new challenges. When immersed in thought, they will sometimes lose touch with the outside world.

The *logician's* four natural inclinations:

- source of life energy: the interior world
- mode of assimilating information: intuition
- decision-making mode: the mind
- lifestyle: spontaneous

Similar personality types:

- the Strategist
- the Innovator
- the Director

Statistical data:

- *logicians* constitute between two and three per cent of the global community;
- men predominate among *logicians* (80 per cent)
- India is an example of a nation corresponding to the *logician's* profile

Find out more!

The Logician. Your Guide to the INTP Personality Type by Jaroslaw Jankowski

The Mentor (INFJ)

Life motto: *The world CAN be a better place!*

Mentors are creative and sensitive. With their gaze fixed firmly on the future, they spot opportunities and potential imperceptible to others. Idealists and visionaries, they are geared towards helping people and are conscientious, responsible and, at one and the same time, courteous, caring and friendly. They strive to understand the mechanisms governing the world and view problems from a wide perspective.

Superb listeners and observers, *mentors* are characterised by their extraordinary empathy, intuition and trust of people and are capable of reading the feelings and emotions of others. They find criticism and conflict difficult to bear and can come across as enigmatic.

The *mentor's* four natural inclinations:

- source of life energy: the interior world
- mode of assimilating information: intuition
- decision-making mode: the heart
- lifestyle: organised

Similar personality types:

- the Idealist
- the Counsellor
- the Enthusiast

Statistical data:

- *mentors* constitute one per cent of the global community and are the most rarely occurring of the sixteen personality types
- women predominate among *mentors* (80 per cent)
- Norway is an example of a nation corresponding to the *mentor's* profile

Find out more!

The Mentor. Your Guide to the INFJ Personality Type
by Jaroslaw Jankowski

The Practitioner (ISTP)

Life motto: *Actions speak louder than words.*

Practitioners are optimistic and spontaneous, with a positive approach to life. Reserved and independent, they hold true to their personal convictions and view external principles and norms with scepticism. They find abstract concepts and solutions for the future tiresome and would far rather roll up their sleeves and get to work on solving tangible and concrete problems.

Adapting well to new places and situations, they enjoy fresh challenges and risks and are capable of keeping a cool head in the face of threats and danger. Their general reticence and extreme reserve when it comes to expressing their opinions mean that other people may often find them impenetrable.

The *practitioner's* four natural inclinations:

- source of life energy: the interior world
- mode of assimilating information: via the senses
- decision-making mode: the mind
- lifestyle: spontaneous

Similar personality types:

- the Inspector
- the Animator
- the Administrator

Statistical data:

- *practitioners* constitute between six and nine per cent of the global community
- men predominate among *practitioners* (60 per cent)
- Singapore is an example of a nation corresponding to the *practitioner's* profile

Find out more!

The Practitioner. Your Guide to the ISTP Personality Type by Jaroslaw Jankowski

The Presenter (ESFP)

Life motto: *Now is the perfect moment!*

Presenters are optimistic, energetic and outgoing, with the ability to enjoy life and have fun to the full. Practical, flexible and spontaneous at one and the same time, they enjoy change and new experiences, coping badly with solitude, stagnation and routine.

With their liking for being at the centre of attention, they are natural-born actors and their speaking abilities arouse the interest and enthusiasm of their listeners. Focused as they are on the present moment, they will sometimes lose sight of their long-term aims and can also have problems with foreseeing the consequences of their actions.

The *presenter's* four natural inclinations:

- source of life energy: the exterior world
- mode of assimilating information: via the senses
- decision-making mode: the heart
- lifestyle: spontaneous

Similar personality types:

- the Advocate
- the Artist
- the Protector

Statistical data:

- *presenters* constitute between eight and thirteen per cent of the global community
- women predominate among *presenters* (60 per cent)
- Brazil is an example of a nation corresponding to the *presenter's* profile

Find out more!

The Presenter. Your Guide to the ESFP Personality Type
by Jaroslaw Jankowski

The Protector (ISFJ)

Life motto: *Your happiness matters to me.*

Protectors are sincere, warm-hearted, unassuming,
trustworthy and extraordinarily loyal. With their ability to
perceive people's needs and their desire to help them, they
will always put others first. Practical, well-organised and
gifted with both an eye and a memory for detail, they are
responsible, hard-working, patient, persevering and capable
of seeing things through to the end.

Protectors set great store by tranquillity, stability and
friendly relations with others and are skilled at building
bridges between people. By the same token, they find
conflict and criticism difficult to bear. Given their powerful
sense of duty and their constant readiness to come to the
aid of others, they can end up being used by people.

The *protector's* four natural inclinations:

- source of life energy: the interior world
- mode of assimilating information: via the senses
- decision-making mode: the heart
- lifestyle: organised

Similar personality types:

- the Artist
- the Advocate
- the Presenter

Statistical data:

- *protectors* constitute between eight and twelve per cent of the global population
- women predominate among *protectors* (70 per cent)
- Sweden is an example of a nation corresponding to the *protector's* profile

Find out more!

The Protector. Your Guide to the ISFJ Personality Type
by Jaroslaw Jankowski

The Strategist (INTJ)

Life motto: *I can certainly improve this.*

Strategists are independent and outstandingly individualistic, with an immense seam of inner energy. Creative, inventive and resourceful, others perceive them as competent, self-assured and, at one and the same time, distant and enigmatic. No matter what they turn their attention to, they will always look at the bigger picture and they have a driving urge to improve the world around them and set it in order.

Well-organised, responsible, critical and demanding, they are difficult to knock off balance – and just as hard to please to the full. Reading the emotions and feelings of others is something they find very problematic.

The *strategist's* four natural inclinations:

- source of life energy: the interior world
- mode of assimilating information: intuition
- decision-making mode: the mind
- lifestyle: organised

Similar personality types:

- the Logician
- the Director
- the Innovator

Statistical data:

- *strategists* constitute between one and two per cent of the global community
- men predominate among *strategists* (80 per cent)
- Finland is an example of a nation corresponding to the *strategist's* profile

Find out more!

The Strategist. Your Guide to the INTJ Personality Type by Jaroslaw Jankowski

Additional information

The four natural inclinations

1. THE DOMINANT SOURCE OF LIFE
   ENERGY

   a. THE EXTERIOR WORLD
      People who draw their energy from
      outside. They need activity and contact
      with others and find being alone for any
      length of time hard to bear.

   b. THE INTERIOR WORLD
      People who draw their energy from their
      inner world. They need quiet and solitude
      and feel drained when they spend any
      length of time in a group.

2. THE DOMINANT MODE OF
    ASSIMILATING INFORMATION

    a. VIA THE SENSES
        People who rely on the five senses and
        are persuaded by facts and evidence. They
        have a liking for methods and practices
        which are tried and tested and prefer
        concrete tasks and are realists who trust in
        experience.

    b. VIA INTUITION
        People who rely on the sixth sense and
        are driven by what they 'feel in their
        bones'. They have a liking for innovative
        solutions and problems of a theoretical
        nature and are characterised by a creative
        approach to their tasks and the ability to
        predict.

3. THE DOMINANT DECISION-MAKING
    MODE

    a. THE MIND
        People who are guided by logic and
        objective principles. They are critical and
        direct in expressing their opinions.

    b. THE HEART
        People who are guided by their feelings
        and values. They long for harmony and
        mutual understanding with others.

4. THE DOMINANT LIFESTYLE

    a. ORGANISED
        People who are conscientious and

organised. They value order and like to operate according to plan.

b.   SPONTANEOUS
People who are spontaneous and value freedom of action. They live for the moment and have no trouble finding their feet in new situations.

The approximate percentage of each personality type in the world population

Personality Type:	Proportion:
• The Administrator (ESTJ):	10-13%
• The Advocate (ESFJ):	10-13%
• The Animator (ESTP):	6-10%
• The Artist (ISFP):	6-9%
• The Counsellor (ENFJ):	3-5 %
• The Director (ENTJ):	2-5%
• The Enthusiast (ENFP):	5-8%
• The Idealist (INFP):	1-4%
• The Innovator (ENTP):	3-5%
• The Inspector (ISTJ):	6-10%
• The Logician (INTP):	2-3%
• The Mentor (INFJ):	ca. 1%
• The Practitioner (ISTP):	6-9%
• The Presenter (ESFP):	8-13%
• The Protector (ISFJ):	8-12%
• The Strategist (INTJ):	1-2%

The approximate percentage of women and men of each personality type in the world population

Personality Type:	Women / Men:
• The Administrator (ESTJ):	40% / 60%
• The Advocate (ESFJ):	70% / 30%
• The Animator (ESTP):	40% / 60%
• The Artist (ISFP):	60% / 40%
• The Counsellor (ENFJ):	80% / 20%
• The Director (ENTJ):	30% / 70%
• The Enthusiast (ENFP):	60% / 40%
• The Idealist (INFP):	60% / 40%
• The Innovator (ENTP):	30% / 70%
• The Inspector (ISTJ):	40% / 60%
• The Logician (INTP):	20% / 80%
• The Mentor (INFJ):	80% / 20%
• The Practitioner (ISTP):	40% / 60%
• The Presenter (ESFP):	60% / 40%
• The Protector (ISFJ):	70% / 30%
• The Strategist (INTJ):	20% / 80%

Recommended publications

The ID16™© Personality Types series

by Jaroslaw Jankowski

The series consists of sixteen books on the individual personality types:

- *The Administrator. Your Guide to the ESTJ Personality Type*
- *The Advocate. Your Guide to the ESFJ Personality Type*
- *The Animator. Your Guide to the ESTP Personality Type*
- *The Artist. Your Guide to the ISFP Personality Type*
- *The Counsellor. Your Guide to the ENFJ Personality Type*
- *The Director. Your Guide to the ENTJ Personality Type*
- *The Enthusiast. Your Guide to the ENFP Personality Type*
- *The Idealist. Your Guide to the INFP Personality Type*
- *The Innovator. Your Guide to the ENTP Personality Type*
- *The Inspector. Your Guide to the ISTJ Personality Type*
- *The Logician. Your Guide to the INTP Personality Type*
- *The Mentor. Your Guide to the INFJ Personality Type*

- *The Practitioner. Your Guide to the ISTP Personality Type*
- *The Presenter. Your Guide to the ESFP Personality Type*
- *The Protector. Your Guide to the ISFJ Personality Type*
- *The Strategist. Your Guide to the INTJ Personality Type*

The series offers a comprehensive description of each of the sixteen types. As you explore them, you will find the answer to a number of crucial questions:

- How do the people who fall within a particular personality type think and what do they feel? How do they make decisions? How do they solve problems? What makes them anxious? What do they fear? What irritates them?
- Which personality types are they happy to encounter on their road through life and which ones do they avoid? What kind of friends, life partners and parents do they make? How are they perceived by others?
- What are their vocational predispositions? What sort of work environments allow them to function most effectively? Which careers best suit their personality type?
- What are their strengths and what do they need to work on? How can they make the most of their potential and avoid pitfalls?
- Which famous people fall within a particular personality type?
- Which nation displays the most features characteristic of a given type?

The books also contain the most essential information about the ID16™© typology.

Who Are You?
The ID16™© Personality Test

by Jaroslaw Jankowski

Which of the sixteen personality types is yours? Are you an energetic and decisive 'administrator'? A sensitive and creative 'artist'? Or a dazzling and analytical 'logician', perhaps?

Who Are You? offers you the ID16 Personality Test, along with an outline of the sixteen personality types, including essential information on their natural inclinations, potential strengths and weaknesses, related types, and an overview of how often each type occurs in the world population. Armed with what you discover, you'll understand yourself and others far better!

Why Are We So Different?
Your Guide to the 16 Personality Types

by Jaroslaw Jankowski

Why are we so very different from one another? Why do we organise our lives in such disparate ways? Why are our modes of assimilating information so varied? Why are our approaches to decision-making so diverse? Why are our forms of relaxing and 'recharging our batteries' so dissimilar?

Your Guide to the 16 Personality Types will help you to understand both yourselves and other people better. It will aid you not only in avoiding any number of traps, but also in making the most of your personal potential, as well as in taking the right decisions about your education and career and in building healthy relationships with others.

The book contains the ID16™© Personality Test, which will enable you to determine your own personality type. It also offers a comprehensive description of each of the sixteen types.

Bibliography

- Arraj, Tyra & Arraj, James: *Tracking the Elusive Human, Volume 1: A Practical Guide to C.G. Jung's Psychological Types, W.H. Sheldon's Body and Temperament Types and Their Integration*, Inner Growth Books, 1988
- Arraj, James: *Tracking the Elusive Human, Volume 2: An Advanced Guide to the Typological Worlds of C. G. Jung, W.H. Sheldon, Their Integration, and the Biochemical Typology of the Future*, Inner Growth Books, 1990
- Berens, Linda V.; Cooper, Sue A.; Ernst, Linda K.; Martin, Charles R.; Myers, Steve; Nardi, Dario; Pearman, Roger R.; Segal, Marci; Smith, Melissa: *A Quick Guide to the 16 Personality Types in Organizations: Understanding Personality Differences in the Workplace*, Telos Publications, 2002
- Geier, John G. & Dorothy E. Downey: *Energetics of Personality*, Aristos Publishing House, 1989
- Hunsaker, Phillip L. & Anthony J. Alessandra: *The Art of Managing People*, Simon and Schuster, 1986

- Jung, Carl Gustav: *Psychological Types (The Collected Works of C. G. Jung, Vol. 6)*, Princeton University Press, 1976
- Kise, Jane A. G.; Stark, David & Krebs Hirsch, Sandra: *LifeKeys: Discover Who You Are*, Bethany House, 2005
- Kroeger, Otto & Thuesen, Janet: *Type Talk or How to Determine Your Personality Type and Change Your Life*, Delacorte Press, 1988
- Lawrence, Gordon: *People Types and Tiger Stripes*, Center for Applications of Psychological Type, 1993
- Lawrence, Gordon: *Looking at Type and Learning Styles*, Center for Applications of Psychological Type, 1997
- Maddi, Salvatore R.: *Personality Theories: A Comparative Analysis*, Waveland, 2001
- Martin, Charles R.: *Looking at Type: The Fundamentals Using Psychological Type To Understand and Appreciate Ourselves and Others*, Center for Applications of Psychological Type, 2001
- Meier C.A.: Personality: *The Individuation Process in the Light of C. G. Jung's Typology*, Daimon Verlag, 2007
- Pearman, Roger R. & Albritton, Sarah: *I'm Not Crazy, I'm Just Not You: The Real Meaning of the Sixteen Personality Types*, Davies-Black Publishing, 1997
- Segal, Marci: Creativity and Personality Type: *Tools for Understanding and Inspiring the Many Voices of Creativity*, Telos Publications, 2001
- Sharp, Daryl: Personality Type: *Jung's Model of Typology*, Inner City Books, 1987
- Spoto, Angelo: *Jung's Typology in Perspective*, Chiron Publications, 1995
- Tannen, Deborah: *You Just Don't Understand*, William Morrow and Company, 1990
- Thomas, Jay C. & Segal, Daniel L.: *Comprehensive Handbook of Personality and Psychopathology, Personality and Everyday Functioning*, Wiley, 2005

- Thomson, Lenore: *Personality Type: An Owner's Manual*, Shambhala, 1998
- Tieger, Paul D. & Barron-Tieger Barbara: *Just Your Type: Create the Relationship You've Always Wanted Using the Secrets of Personality Type*, Little, Brown and Company, 2000
- Von Franz, Marie-Louise & Hillman, James: *Lectures on Jung's Typology*, Continuum International Publishing Group, 1971

About the Author

Jaroslaw Jankowski holds a Master of Education degree from Nicolaus Copernicus University in Toruń, Poland and an MBA from the Brennan School of Business at the Dominican University in River Forest, Illinois, USA. The research and development director of an international NGO and an entrepreneur, he is also involved in voluntary work. He is not only committed to promoting knowledge about personality types, but is also the creator of ID16$^{TM©}$, an independent personality typology based on the theory developed by Carl Gustav Jung.

Putting the Reader first.

An Author Campaign Facilitated by ALLi.

Lightning Source UK Ltd.
Milton Keynes UK
UKOW03f2345250417
299865UK00002B/48/P